Greta Thunberg
Climate Activist

by Elizabeth Neuenfeldt

BLASTOFF!
2
READERS

BELLWETHER MEDIA • MINNEAPOLIS, MN

Blastoff! Readers are carefully developed by literacy experts to build reading stamina and move students toward fluency by combining standards-based content with developmentally appropriate text.

 Level 1 provides the most support through repetition of high-frequency words, light text, predictable sentence patterns, and strong visual support.

 Level 2 offers early readers a bit more challenge through varied sentences, increased text load, and text-supportive special features.

 Level 3 advances early-fluent readers toward fluency through increased text load, less reliance on photos, advancing concepts, longer sentences, and more complex special features.

★ **Blastoff! Universe**

Reading Level

Grade **K**

Grades **1–3**

Grade **4**

This edition first published in 2022 by Bellwether Media, Inc.

No part of this publication may be reproduced in whole or in part without written permission of the publisher. For information regarding permission, write to Bellwether Media, Inc., Attention: Permissions Department, 6012 Blue Circle Drive, Minnetonka, MN 55343.

Library of Congress Cataloging-in-Publication Data

Names: Neuenfeldt, Elizabeth, author.
Title: Greta Thunberg : climate activist / by Elizabeth Neuenfeldt.
Description: Minneapolis, MN : Bellwether Media, Inc., 2022. | Series: Women leading the way | Includes bibliographical references and index. | Audience: Ages 5-8 | Audience: Grades 2-3 | Summary: "Relevant images match informative text in this introduction to Greta Thunberg. Intended for students in kindergarten through third grade"–Provided by publisher.
Identifiers: LCCN 2021041246 (print) | LCCN 2021041247 (ebook) | ISBN 9781644875933 (library binding) | ISBN 9781648346682 (paperback) | ISBN 9781648346040 (ebook)
Subjects: LCSH: Thunberg, Greta, 2003–Juvenile literature. | Environmentalists–Sweden–Biography–Juvenile literature.
Classification: LCC GE56.T55 N48 2022 (print) | LCC GE56.T55 (ebook) | DDC 363.738/74092 [B]–dc23
LC record available at https://lccn.loc.gov/2021041246
LC ebook record available at https://lccn.loc.gov/2021041247

Editor: Betsy Rathburn   Designer: Gabriel Hilger

Printed in the United States of America, North Mankato, MN.

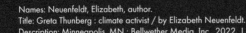

Table of Contents

Who Is Greta Thunberg?

Greta Thunberg is an **activist**. She fights to stop **climate change**.

She wants to save the planet!

"CHANGE IS COMING, WHETHER YOU LIKE IT OR NOT." (2019)

#FridaysForFuture

Greta was born in 2003 in Stockholm, Sweden.

Stockholm
Greta's hometown

Sweden

N
W   E
S

Greta and her father

Young Greta became upset about climate change. Her family lowered their **carbon footprint**. But Greta wanted to do more.

Greta striking for climate change

In high school, Greta began to **strike**. She skipped school to **protest**.

She wanted the government to help stop climate change.

Greta Thunberg Profile

Birthday: January 3, 2003

Hometown: Stockholm, Sweden

Field: climate activism

Schooling: high school

Influences:
- Rosa Parks (civil rights activist)
- Malala Yousafzai (education activist)

Greta continued to strike every week. Kids around the world joined her.

Fridays for
Future protest

The protest became known
as Fridays for Future.
It continues today!

Greta's work influenced adults, too.

She spoke to many world leaders. She asked them to make laws to stop climate change.

Greta at a climate change meeting

"I HAVE LEARNED THAT YOU ARE NEVER TOO SMALL TO MAKE A DIFFERENCE." (2018)

G. THUNBERG

Greta speaking about climate change

Not everyone liked Greta. They thought she was too young. Some people made fun of her for having **Asperger's syndrome**.

But Greta kept fighting!

Greta won **awards** for speaking out.

Greta accepting a Climate Protection Award

16

Greta also formed a **foundation**. It finds ways to take care of the earth.

person receiving a
COVID-19 vaccine

Greta helped during the
COVID-19 pandemic. Not
everyone could get **vaccines**.
Greta did not think this was fair.

Her foundation gave almost $120,000 to help people get vaccines!

Greta Thunberg Timeline

2018 — Greta protests outside of the Swedish parliament

SEPTEMBER 2019 — Greta speaks to world leaders at the 2019 UN Climate Action Summit

DECEMBER 2019 — Greta wins the 2019 Right Livelihood Award for her protests

2020 — Greta forms the Greta Thunberg Foundation

2021 — The Greta Thunberg Foundation gives almost $120,000 to help people get vaccines

Greta still works
to stop climate change.
She **inspires** people
everywhere.

Greta shows that
young people can
change the world!

Glossary

activist—a person who believes in taking action to make changes in laws or society

Asperger's syndrome—a condition that changes how the brain develops and affects how a person speaks and acts

awards—rewards or prizes that are given for a job well done

carbon footprint—the amount of carbon dioxide given off by people's activities; a carbon footprint can be lowered by driving less and recycling.

climate change—a human-caused change in Earth's weather due to warming temperatures

COVID-19 pandemic—an outbreak of the COVID-19 virus starting in December 2019 that led to millions of deaths and shutdowns around the world

foundation—a group that gives money in order to do something that helps society

inspires—gives someone an idea about what to do or create

protest—to show strong disagreement with or disapproval of something

strike—to stop working or going to school in order to make changes happen

vaccines—substances that are put into people or animals to protect them against certain diseases

To Learn More

AT THE LIBRARY

Leaf, Christina. *Rachel Carson: Environmentalist*. Minneapolis, Minn.: Bellwether Media, 2019.

Rose, Rachel. *Greta Thunberg: Teen Climate Activist*. Minneapolis, Minn.: Bearport Publishing, 2021.

Winter, Jeanette. *Our House Is on Fire: Greta Thunberg's Call to Save The Planet*. New York, N.Y.: Beach Lane Books, 2019.

ON THE WEB

FACTSURFER

Factsurfer.com gives you a safe, fun way to find more information.

1. Go to www.factsurfer.com.

2. Enter "Greta Thunberg" into the search box and click 🔍.

3. Select your book cover to see a list of related content.

PROTECT OUR PLANET

Index

The images in this book are reproduced through the courtesy of: Jasper Chamber/ Alamy, front cover (Greta), pp. 8-9; FooTToo, front cover (background), pp. 10-11 (bottom); Inside Creative House, p. 3 (sign), 23 (sign); NPeter, p. 4 (Earth); lev radin, pp. 4-5; Spencer Platt/ Getty Images, pp. 6-7; Antonello Marangi, p. 9; Andrew Benton/ Alamy, pp. 10-11 (top); Pablo Blazquez Dominguez/ Getty Images, p. 12 (inset); Leon Neal/ Getty Images, pp. 12-13, 15; picture alliance/ Getty Images, pp. 14-15; REUTERS/ Alamy, p. 16; Timon Goertz, pp. 16-17; Jim West/ Alamy, pp. 18-19; Gregrobby, p. 20 (inset); dpa picture alliance/ Alamy, pp. 20-21.